Written by Beatrice Fontanel
Illustrated by Anne Logvinoff

Specialist adviser:
Sarah Heath,
M. Phil Conservation Policy

ISBN 1 85103 173 1
First published 1993 in the United Kingdom
by Moonlight Publishing Ltd,
36 Stratford Road, London W8
Translated by Sarah Matthews

© 1989 by Editions Gallimard
English text © 1993 by Moonlight Publishing Ltd
Printed in Italy by Editoriale Libraria

POCKET • WORLDS

Animals of the Night

What goes on
in the countryside
while we're asleep?

Dusk is falling over the countryside.

The sky glows deep red as the sun sinks down. Daisies close up their petals for the night, while evening primrose flowers unfurl theirs. Animals are snuggling down to sleep in their nests and burrows, but other animals are beginning to stir and wake up. Animals that are active at night are called nocturnal animals.

One of the first to appear is the badger, carefully sniffing the night air at the entrance to his set.

Some fish settle down to sleep in the weeds.

When he is sure that it's safe, the badger steps out and pads about his business, rummaging in the earth with his huge paws, searching for worms.
A badger can eat up to two hundred worms in a single night.

Hedgehogs set out to hunt and explore.

The barn owl is hungry after sleeping through the day.
It will be up all night hunting.

Nature never rests.

Animals sleep and wake at different times.
Some are awake only part of the night.
Others doze on and off all night through.

Stoats hunt by day and by night. When it's very cold, they build
up a store so that they don't have to venture out.

A raccoon is up all night. An orange swift moth goes out at dusk.

What do all these animals do in the night?

Some hunt, some build their nests and burrows, some feed, some look for a partner to mate with, and some, like the badger, clean out their burrows.

Caterpillars quietly chew their way into the leaves, while moths flutter through the night, each species at a different time.

10

Like many animals which hunt at night, barn owls move swiftly and silently.

A ghostly figure sweeps over the fields – its white feathers catch the moonlight. **It is a barn owl.**

Barn owls are not afraid of people, and often nest in belfries and farm buildings. They have a haunting, screeching cry.

They eat voles, mice, fish, frogs, lizards and other small animals. Even on the darkest night their eyes can spot the slightest movement and their sharp hearing can pick up a small rustle in the grass. Wings spread, claws outstretched, they swoop down on their prey.

Tawny owl	**Long-eared owl**	**Little owl**	**Barred owl**

The stars shine clear and bright in the desert sky.

Down amongst the rocks and pebbles, and along the surface of the sand, all sorts of animals creep soundlessly about. Rattlesnakes set out after the warm-blooded creatures that they feed on, scenting their warmth through special openings in their noses.

A scorpion is lying in ambush, its feet
resting lightly on the ground, ready to feel
the slightest vibration. When it feels its prey
coming, it turns towards it,
pincers at the ready, and
pounces on it.

The fennec fox, its huge ears twitching,
hunts round about the oases
under cover of dark.

**In the black shadows under
the trees, bats flit to and fro.**
They find their way
by ultra-sound.

They give out tiny cries, so high our human
ears cannot hear them. The sounds bounce
off the trees and branches round them,
and are picked up by the bats' ultra-sound
sense. This means that, even on the darkest
night, they know where trees and branches
are, and never bump into them. There are
fourteen different kinds of bat in Britain.
They all eat moths, mosquitoes and flies.

Bats have only one baby a year. The mother carries her little
one with her, clinging on to her fur. Bats are the only mammal
that can fly.

Bats drink a great deal,
even when they are flying.
They dip down and
skim a mouthful
from a lake, or lick
the dew from
a leaf as they
fly past.

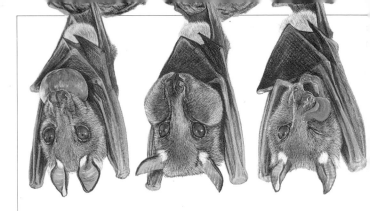

During the heat of the day, in Africa and Asia, thousands of fruit bats hang upside down to rest in cool caves or in trees. When night falls, they take to the air in huge, swirling clouds, darkening the sky. They are searching for figs, mangoes, bananas and other soft fruit. They fly slowly but powerfully; their wings have a span of one metre.

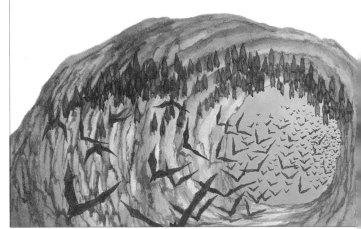

Fruit bats enjoy sucking the sweet nectar from flowers.

At dawn they fly back to their cave to roost, but they take a long time to settle down. They squabble and fidget and chatter until they finally fall silent, clinging on to the roof and walls with their feet, and wrapping their leathery wings round them like a sleeping bag.

In the Nye Cave, in Texas, USA, several million bats live in one enormous colony. When they leave the cave at night, it looks as if a plume of black smoke is rising into the sky. If they are disturbed during the day time, thousands upon thousands of them fly about excitedly, without even knocking into each other!

The hammer-headed bat, found in tropical forests, has a strange, spoon-shaped nose! This helps it collect pollen and nectar from flowers in the forest.

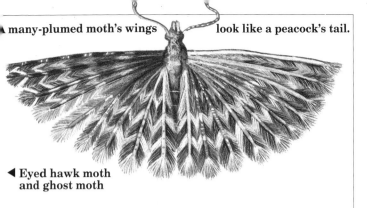

A many-plumed moth's wings look like a peacock's tail.

◀ Eyed hawk moth and ghost moth

Have you ever heard a quiet fluttering against your window-pane on a summer's night? It is the sound of a moth knocking against the glass, attracted by the light inside the room. Moths can fly quite silently, flitting out of the way of predators like bats and owls. They have special ears, too, which can pick up the ultra-sound of the animals who would like to eat them.

The Moon moth, elegant as a prince

Narrow-bordered bee hawk moths live in Africa and Asia.

On a dark and moonless night, you may suddenly see hundreds of tiny green lights winking among the leaves.

They are glow-worms and fireflies.

In order to let each other know where they are, so that couples can meet and mate, male and female glow-worms shine a light in their tails. The tips of their tails, which are covered with fine, almost transparent skin, contain a substance which glows in the dark.

Male glow-worms can fly, but the females cannot. They attract attention by clinging on to a leaf and curling their shining tails upwards.

The eggs and grubs of fireflies give off light as well. Frogs like eating them, and until they have finished digesting them, they start to glow too!

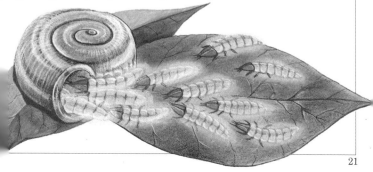

We can smell the damp earth and the scent of plants hanging on the night air.

But there are other scents which are too delicate and subtle for our noses to smell.

Some female insects spray tiny amounts of scent into the air so that the males can find them. The scent may smell of, pineapple or of chocolate. Tropical water-bugs smell of vanilla.

Moths, attracted by the scent of the night flowers, suck up their nectar through their proboscis.

◀ Some moths in Thailand drink the tears of the banteng.

Using its feathery antennae, the silkmoth can pick up the scent of a female from several kilometres away.

As night falls, water boatmen step across the surface of the water between the reeds. **Then the frogs and toads start their evening serenade.**

On one side of the marshes, some frogs start calling. Soon others return their cry. It is not long before there is a whole concert of cries.

own by the water-lilies, you might hear
e fluting cry of the rare midwife toad.
o in the reeds, a yellow-bellied toad cries.
eastern Europe, there are fire-bellied
ads which have a thudding,
llowing call.

A thousand metres below the surface of the sea, it is always dark. Some fish and squid down there are phosphorescent.

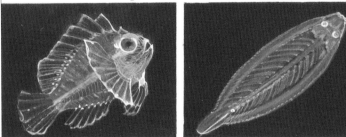

Fish with transparent skins have a greater chance of escaping from the predators waiting for them in the dark.

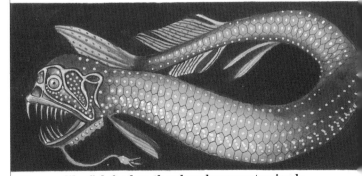

Dragon-like fish feed on the phosphorescent animals, following them as they make their nightly swims.

The moon has risen over the dancing waves, but what is happening down below? **A great many fish are at their most active at dusk and at dawn.**

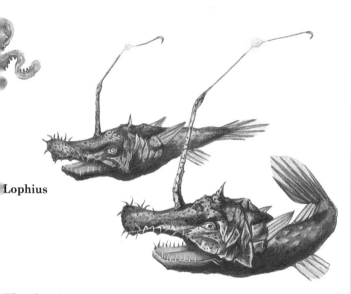

Lophius

The lophius has another name. It is called the angler fish because of the curious rod which sticks up from the top of its nose. The rod has a luminous float on it which the angler fish uses to attract its prey.

Lantern-fish, which are most active at night, have luminous organs too. They shake them to distract their predators.

Exotic animals of the night

All over the world, curious-looking animals creep out as night falls.

The African aardvark

Aardvarks come out at night and snuffle across the African plains in search of ants and termites to eat.

In Argentina, in South America, a kind of tiny armadillo with pink armour across its back, called the pink fairy armadillo, comes creeping out of its burrow at dusk.

The spiny echidna, or ant-eater, lives
in New Guinea. It lives in hollows in trees
or down among the roots. It comes out
at night to root through the forest floor,
looking for insects to eat.

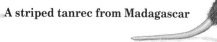

A striped tanrec from Madagascar

The striped tanrec is bigger than a rat.
When it is disturbed it makes a clicking
sound by vibrating a tuft of spines
in the middle of its back.

An Australian bandicoot. It sleeps
all day long, burrowed down
in the soil well away from
the heat of the sun.

Sunrise

The pigeons start to coo. The finches and the warblers each try to sing louder than the others. The tits pick and preen at their feathers. A few early bees are beginning to buzz around the cow-parsley.

It is time for some animals to go to bed. Moths hide from the light in cracks and hollows. A fox, tired after its night's hunting, brings back food for the young in its den.

Some animals are only just waking up. Dormice and shrews start snuffling about in search of food. Squirrels cautiously poke their noses out of their nests.

A mole makes a brief appearance above ground at dawn, before plunging down to dig more tunnels in its hunt for worms.

As soon as the sun is up, the rabbits will scurry back to their burrow to hide.

If you go for a walk in the fields or through the forest, can you see the tracks that have been left by the animals of the night? Keep your eyes open and walk very slowly, or you won't see everything that is there!

a hedgehog...

Tracks left by a cat...

a badger...

a fox and a dog.

There may be tracks left in damp soil, wild fruit that has been gnawed at, some hairs caught on the bark of a tree...

Owls get rid of the bones and fur of the animals they have eaten, spitting them out in neat bundles called pellets.

All around you there are fascinating clues to the different dramas that have happened while you slept.

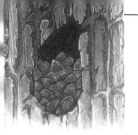

This hazelnut has been gnawed by a field-mouse and this pine-cone has been stripped by a vole.

A busy squirrel has stored up lots of acorns in a hole in a tree. A moth has left tracks on the underside of a leaf.

Badgers leave their droppings in a hole they dig outside the entrance to the set.

Can you tell who lives in a burrow by the shape of the entrance? Is it a fox or a badger?

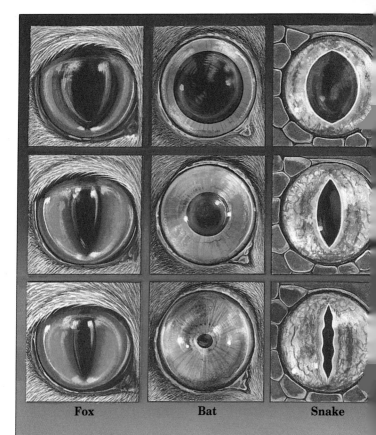

Fox   **Bat**   **Snake**

The night has a thousand eyes...

Animals who live and hunt at night often
need especially effective eyes. Because there
is little light, their eyes are made so that
they can catch and use even the slightest
glow. Bright light hurts them, and their
pupils will close to pinpoints or the thinnest
of slits to keep it out.

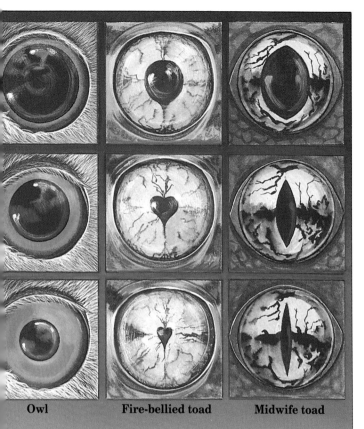

Owl   **Fire-bellied toad**   **Midwife toad**

Even when the night seems black and dark to us, there is still enough light for an owl to hunt by. Snakes do not have pupils, but their eyes are protected by a transparent skin. Frogs' eyes are particularly good at spotting movement: a reed waving in the wind, an insect, an enemy coming towards them...

Index

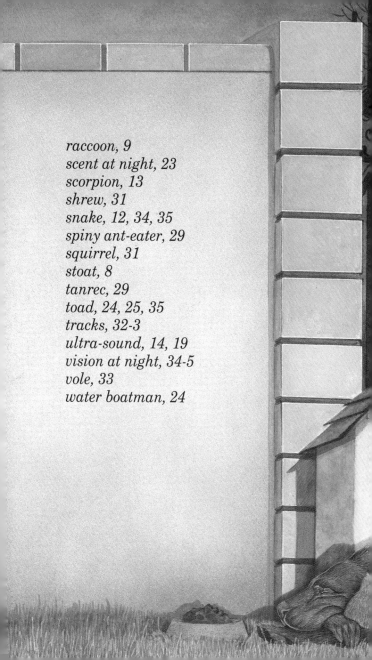